The ABC's
OF HANDLING MONEY GOD'S WAY

MOODY PUBLISHERS

CHICAGO

What's Inside

© Copyright 1998 by Crown Ministries, Inc.

Unless otherwise noted, Scripture quotation are from the *New American Standard Bible,* copyright 1960, 1962, 1963, 1968, 1971, 1973, 1975, 1975, 1977 by the Lockman Foundation.

Verses identified as NIV are taken from the *Holy Bible: New International Version,* copyright 1973, 1978, 1984, by the International Bible Society. Used by permission of Zondervan Bible Publishers.

Verses identified as LB as taken from *The Living Bible*, 1971 by Tyndale House Publishers. Used by permission.

Verses identified as (Amplified) are from the *Amplified New Testament,* copyright 1954, 1958, 1987 by the Lockman Foundation. Used by permission.

Scripture quotations marked (NLT) are taken from the *Holy Bible, New Living Translation,* copyright © 1996. Used by permission of Tyndale House Publishers, Inc., Wheaton, Illinois 60189. All rights reserved.

ISBN-13: 978-0-8024-3152-3   ISBN-10: 0-8024-3152-6

5 7 9 10 8 6 4   Printed in Italy

This fun book belongs to:

_____

Chapter 1

The Wish

The children were sad. It was raining and they could not play outside.

"I wish we had a puppy," Elizabeth said. "A puppy would help to make rainy days fun."

Elizabeth's friends, Paul, Juan and Sarah agreed.

Elizabeth's mother, Mrs. Day, said, "A puppy does sound like fun. But puppies cost money. And then you have to buy a collar, leash and dog food."

"I did not know puppies cost money," said Paul with a surprised look on his face.

"Mom, would you help us find ways to earn money?" asked Elizabeth.

"I will help you, if you do something for me," said Mrs. Day.

"What do you want us to do?" asked Sarah.

Mrs. Day picked up her Bible. She said, "I want you to find out what God says about money."

Sarah's eyes grew large. "Does God talk about money?" she asked.

"Yes," said Mrs. Day smiling. "God loves you. He wants to help you use money in the best way. We will have twelve lessons. In each lesson you will answer some questions. And we will learn a Bible verse."

"That will be fun!" said the children.

"When can we start?" asked Juan.

"Right now," answered Mrs. Day. "First, let me

tell you about the Bible. It is called the Word of God. Second Timothy 3:16 says *the whole Bible was given to us . . . by God and is useful to teach us what is true* (LB). Psalm 119:105 tells us, *Your word is a lamp to my feet and light to my path.* Lights help us see at night. And the Bible helps us see what God wants us to do with money."

"Do you think we can earn enough money to buy a puppy?" asked Juan.

"I sure do," said Mrs. Day.

"Look, it stopped raining!" shouted Sarah.

"We have finished lesson one," said Mrs. Day. "Do you want to play outside now?"

"Yes!" the kids shouted as they ran outside and jumped in a big puddle.

Learn this verse.

"Your word is a lamp to my feet and a light to my path."

(Psalm 119:105, NIV)

Answer these Questions.

Read 2 Timothy 3:16.

What does this verse say about the Bible?

_____

_____

Read Hebrews 12:4.

What does this verse say about the Word of God?

_____

_____

Why is the Bible called the Word of God?

_____

_____

Things to do...

What is the name of each coin? How many cents is each coin worth?

Name?   How many cents?

_____   _____

_____   _____

_____   _____

_____   _____

If you do not have a Bible, please get one.

Write your prayer on page 77

Chapter 2

Who Owns The Ball?

"It's mine! You can't have it," said Paul. He took the ball away from Juan.

"Paul, do you know who owns the ball?" asked Mrs. Day.

"I do. I bought it with my money." said Paul.

"Let's find out who really owns the ball," said Mrs. Day. She called the children together. "Elizabeth, will you read 1 Chronicles 29:11?"

Elizabeth opened her Bible and read, *"Everything in the heavens and earth is yours, O Lord."*

"Does that mean God owns my toys?" asked Sarah.

"Does He even own my ball?" asked Paul.

"Let's read more to find out," replied Mrs. Day. She asked Paul to read 1 Corinthians 10:26.

"The earth is the Lord's, and everything in it," read Paul. "God does own everything, even my ball."

"Now listen to what else God says," Mrs. Day continued. *"All the animals of field and forest are mine! The cattle on a thousand hills! And all the birds upon the mountains!*" (Psalm 50:10, TLB).

Elizabeth exclaimed, "God even owns all the puppies!"

"Let's pray and ask Him to bring us one," said Juan excitedly.

"That is a good idea, Juan," Mrs. Day replied. Everyone bowed their heads and prayed for a puppy.

"In our next lesson," said Mrs. Day, "we will learn what the Lord wants us to do with our money and our things."

"I know something God wants me to do now", said Paul. "Take God's ball, Juan. You can play with it." Paul handed the ball to Juan.

Learn this verse.

"Everything in the heavens and earth is yours, O Lord."

(1 Chronicles 29:11, TLB)

Answer these Questions.

Read Psalm 24:1. What does God own?

_____

_____

Read Psalm 50:10-12. List the animals in these verses that God owns.

_____

_____

_____

Things to do...

Color some of the things in your room that God owns.

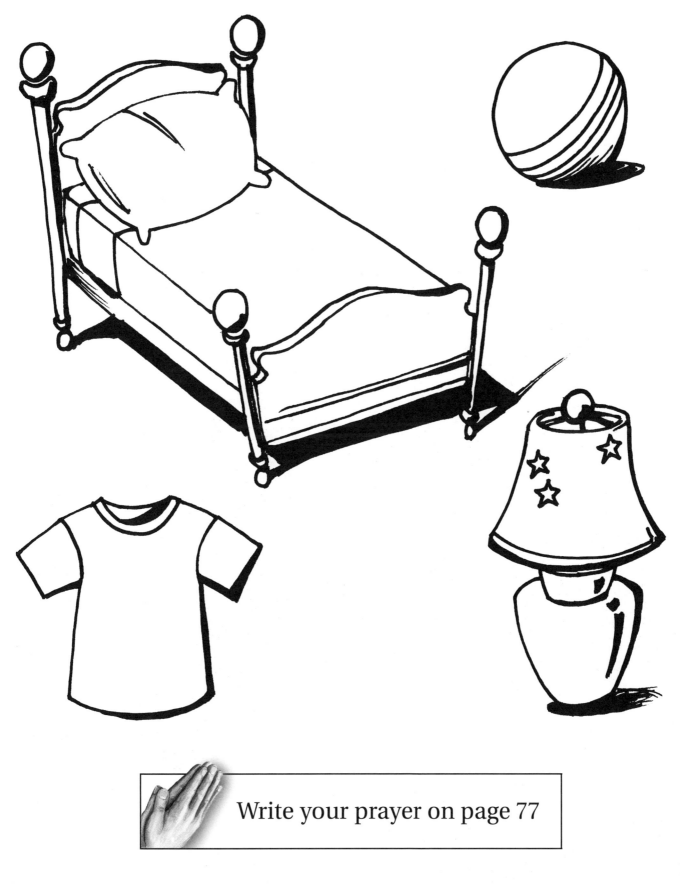

Write your prayer on page 77

Chapter 3

You Are A Steward

The kids ran into the house as it began to rain.

"Everyone bring your Bible," said Mrs. Day.

"Let's do the next lesson. Paul, please read 1 Corinthians 4:2."

Paul read, *"It is required in stewards that a man be found faithful.* What is a steward?" he asked.

"A steward takes care of someone else's things," replied Mrs. Day. "God owns everything. And we take care of God's things. The verse you read said we are to be faithful. What is a faithful steward?"

"I know, Mom," said Elizabeth. "A faithful steward takes good care of God's things."

"That's right, Elizabeth," replied Mrs. Day. "There was a faithful steward in the Bible. He took good care of animals. When he lived, it rained for 40 days without stopping. Does anyone know His name?"

"Noah," Juan said. "Noah took care of lots of animals in the ark."

"That was a lot of work," groaned Paul. "Think about feeding all those animals."

"Yes, it was hard work," said Mrs. Day. "But Noah and his family were faithful stewards of those animals."

"I can't wait to be a faithful steward of our puppy," said Sarah.

"I know," said Mrs. Day. "But how can you be a faithful steward before you get the puppy?"

"We can take good care of our toys, our clothes and our money," said Paul.

"Mom, when are we going to earn money to buy the puppy?" asked Elizabeth.

"In the next lesson we will learn what God says about work," said Mrs. Day. "Then we will decide how to earn money."

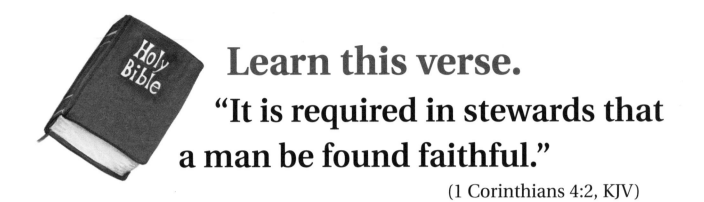

Learn this verse.

"It is required in stewards that a man be found faithful."

(1 Corinthians 4:2, KJV)

Answer these Questions.

Read 1 Corinthians 4:2. What does this verse mean to you?

_____

_____

_____

What does the word steward mean?

_____

_____

_____

What are some of the ways you can be a faithful steward?

_____

_____

_____

Things to do...

Color these children who are being faithful stewards. Tell your teacher what each child is doing.

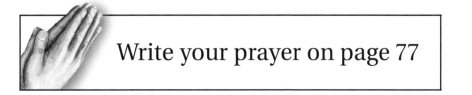 Write your prayer on page 77

Chapter 4

Working For The Lord

The kids were excited. They were going to learn what God says about work. They would talk about how to earn money to buy a puppy.

"Let me tell you a Bible story. It is about a boy named David," Mrs. Day began. "David took care of his father's sheep. He fed them. David watched the sheep so none of them got lost."

"It must be hard work to take care of sheep," said Juan.

"Yes, work can be hard," replied Mrs. Day. "But the Lord wants us to work hard. Paul, read Ecclesiastes 9:10."

"Sure," said Paul. *"Whatever your hand finds to do, do it with all your might."*

"Does this mean we should work hard at school?" asked Juan.

"What about my chores at home?" asked Sarah.

"Yes, we are to work hard at school and at home," said Mrs. Day.

"Mom, can we talk now about earning money to buy the puppy?" asked Elizabeth.

"Yes," replied Mrs. Day. "I talked to your parents. We made a list of jobs you can do."

The kids looked at the list.

"I am going to fold the clothes and help wash the kitchen floor," said Elizabeth.

"I am going to take out the trash," said Paul.

"I will help my mom clean the dishes," said Juan.

"I thought I was too little to work," said Sarah. "But I can empty trash cans."

"Remember to work hard at these jobs," said Mrs. Day. "And in our next lesson we will learn the first thing God wants us to do the with money we earn."

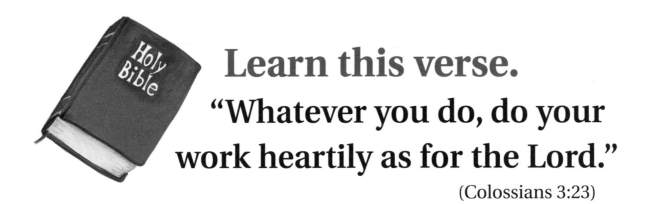

Learn this verse.

"Whatever you do, do your work heartily as for the Lord."

(Colossians 3:23)

Answer these Questions.

Read Colossians 3:23-24. What do these verses say about work?

_____

_____

Read 2 Thessalonians 3:8-9. What do these verses say about working hard?

_____

_____

Are you a hard worker?

_____

_____

Things to do...

Trace one of your hands on this page. Hands can do many different jobs. Draw a line from your hand to the things you do to help at home.

Write your prayer on page 77

27

Chapter 5

Giving

"I made a lot of money this week!" shouted Paul.

Elizabeth and Juan said, "We did too!"

Only Sarah was quiet.

"All of you are working hard," said Mrs. Day. "Juan, read Acts 20:35. It will tell you the first thing God wants you to do with your money."

"It is more blessed to give than to receive," read Juan. "But I worked so hard," said Juan. "Why should I give money away?"

"God wants you to give some of it," said Mrs. Day kindly. "He will bless you in many ways when you give."

"How much should we give?" asked Paul.

"A tithe is a good place to start," said Mrs. Day. "A tithe is 10 percent. You give one penny out of every ten pennies you receive. You can give more if you want."

"Mom, who should we give to?" asked Elizabeth.

"First, give to your church," answered Mrs. Day. "The Lord also wants us to give to poor people. Proverbs 28:27 says, *He who gives to the poor will never want.*"

Sarah began to softly cry.

"Sarah, why are you crying?" Mrs. Day asked.

"I earned only ten pennies. I cannot give much," Sarah said.

"Does anyone know a Bible story that might help Sarah?" asked Mrs. Day.

"How about the story of the poor widow?" said Elizabeth. "Jesus was watching people give. Some people gave a lot of money. Then a poor widow gave only two small coins. Jesus was very happy with the widow. She gave all she had."

"Very good, Elizabeth," said Mrs. Day. "That story is found in Mark 12:42-44.

"Now, I want to give each of you a jar," she said. "The word **Giving** is on the jars. When you get money, put what you are going to give in the jar.

"In the next lesson we will learn about saving."

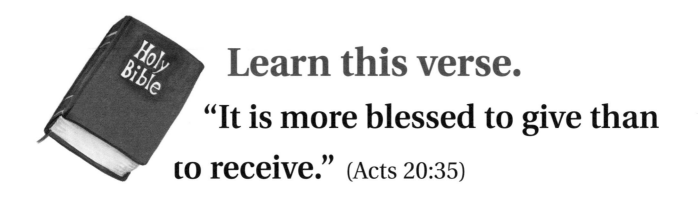

Learn this verse.

"It is more blessed to give than to receive." (Acts 20:35)

Answer these Questions.

Read Acts 20:35. What do you think this verse means?

_____

_____

_____

How much money should you give?

_____

_____

What does the word tithe mean?

_____

_____

Things to do...

Get a jar or box and write **Giving** on it. Put the money you want to give in this jar or box.

Pretend you have earned ten dimes. Circle in red the dimes you will give.

Pray for the Lord to use the money you give to help your church and the poor.

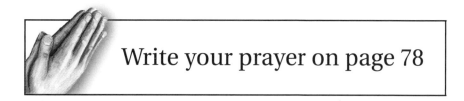

Write your prayer on page 78

Chapter 6

Saving

"God calls ants wise," said Mrs. Day.

"But ants are so small." said Sarah.

"How can they be smart?"

"Good question, Sarah," replied Mrs. Day. "Elizabeth, please read Proverbs 30:24-25."

Elizabeth opened her Bible. She read, *"Ants are extremely wise . . . they store up their food in the summer."*

"What does that verse mean?" asked Mrs. Day.

"Ants are smart because they save," said Juan.

"That is right," said Mrs. Day. "Proverbs 21:20 says, *the wise man saves."*

"Mom, did people in the Bible save?" asked Elizabeth.

"Joseph saved," replied Mrs. Day. "God told Joseph that there would be seven good years with a lot of food. Then seven bad years would follow with no food. Joseph saved food during the seven good years. There was food to eat during the seven bad years because he saved."

"I am going to give you a gift to help you save," said Mrs. Day. She took out four jars. Each jar was painted with the word **Saving**.

"Every time you get money, what are you going to do with it?" asked Mrs. Day.

"The first thing I am going to do is put some of the money in the Giving jar," said Juan. "Then I will put some money in the Saving jar."

"Juan, that is very good," said Mrs. Day.

"We should save for the puppy," said Paul.

The other kids agreed. They all put some of their money in their Saving jar.

"I also want you to learn about a savings account," said Mrs. Day. "Ask your parents to take you to a bank so you can open a savings account. The bank will keep your money safe. The bank will give you more money than you put in bank. It is called interest.

"When you come for the next lesson bring your two jars and your money."

Learn this verse.

"**The wise man saves for the future; the foolish man spends whatever he gets.**" (Proverbs 21:20, LB)

Answer these Questions.

Read Proverbs 30:24-25. What do these verses say about ants saving?

_____

_____

_____

_____

Do you save money? How much money should you save?

_____

_____

When a bank pays you interest, what does that mean?

_____

_____

Things to do...

Get a jar or box and write **Saving** on it. Put the money you are saving in the jar or box.

Pretend you have earned ten dimes. First circle in red the dimes you will give. Then circle in green the dimes you will save.

With your parent's help, open a savings account at a bank.

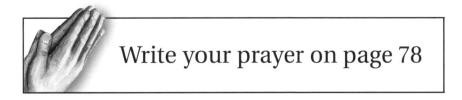

Write your prayer on page 78

39

Chapter 7

The Doll

"I saw the prettiest doll on television," Sarah exclaimed. "I want to buy it right now!"

"Before we talk about the doll," said Mrs. Day kindly, "I want to give each of you a Spending jar."

41

"Now we have three jars," said Juan. "One is for Giving. One is for Saving. And one is for Spending. Let's put our money in the jars."

Sarah counted the money in her Spending jar. "I don't have enough money to buy the doll now," she said sadly.

"I know you are sad because you cannot buy the doll," said Mrs. Day. "Let me read Philippians 4:11. *For I have learned how to get along happily whether I have much or little.* What do you think that verse means?"

Paul answered, "Does it mean we should be happy with what we have?"

"Yes," answered Mrs. Day. "The Bible says we can be happy when we are thankful for what we have already."

"Does that mean we should not want new things?" asked Elizabeth.

"You may want new things," said Mrs. Day. "But you should decide what you want the most."

"I want the doll," said Sarah. "But I want the puppy more."

"So, what will you do?" asked Mrs. Day.

"Save my money," answered Sarah.

"Very good, Sarah," said Mrs. Day nodding. "All of you want to buy the puppy. Count how much money you have to buy the puppy."

They poured their money on the floor and counted it.

"How can we can find out if we have enough money to buy a puppy?" asked Elizabeth excitedly.

"Tomorrow we will go to the pet store and find out," said Mrs. Day smiling.

Learn this verse.

"**For I have learned how to get along happily whether I have much or little.**" (Philippians 4:11, NLT)

Answer these Questions.

Read Philippians 4:11-13. What do you think these verses mean?

_____

_____

_____

_____

List three things you want to buy.
Write down how much each one costs.

1_____ $_____

2_____ $_____

3_____ $_____

Draw a star next to the thing you want to buy first.

Things to do...

Get a jar or box and write **Spending** on it. Put the money you want to spend in the Spending jar or box.

Pretend you have earned ten dimes. First circle in red the dimes you will give. Then circle in green the dimes you will save. Then circle in blue the dimes you can spend.

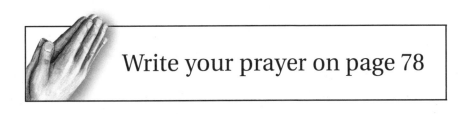

Write your prayer on page 78

Chapter 8

Debt

Look at the puppies!" Elizabeth said

excitedly as they looked in the window of the

pet store.

There were seven little puppies looking back. Their little tails were wagging.

"They are so cute," said Paul. "Let's go in and ask if we can hold them."

Soon each child was holding a puppy. The puppies were licking the children's faces.

"I can't believe how soft they are," said Paul.

The man at the pet store asked. "Would you like to buy a puppy?"

"Yes!" The kids answered.

"How much does a puppy cost?" asked Paul. The man told him. "We don't have that much money," said Paul sadly.

"Maybe you can borrow the money to buy

the puppy," said the man.

"Can we borrow the money, Mom, please?" asked Elizabeth.

"When you borrow money you go into debt," said Mrs. Day in a concerned voice.

"What is debt?" asked Juan.

"Debt is when you borrow money," answered Mrs. Day.

"Does the Bible say anything about debt?" Sarah asked.

"Yes," answered Mrs. Day. "In Romans 13:8 it says, *Keep out of debt.*"

"Then I think we should save until we have enough money to buy a puppy," said Juan.

"We should keep praying. Maybe God will give us the puppy in a special way," added Elizabeth.

The four friends agreed to save and pray.

Learn this verse.

"Keep out of debt."

(Romans 13:8, Amplified)

Answer these Questions.

Read Romans 13:8.

What does this verse tell us about borrowing money?

_____

_____

_____

What is debt?

_____

_____

_____

Things to do...

STAY OUT OF DEBT

Read the sentences with your teacher.
Circle the word that will keep you out of debt.

1. The Bible tells us that we should not

   OWE SAVE money.

2. I can BORROW SAVE money for a new toy.

3. I will try to EMPTY FILL my saving jar.

Write your prayer on page 78

Chapter 9

What is Counsel?

Elizabeth was sitting on her mom's lap when the kids arrived. "Come in," said Elizabeth happily.

"Why are you smiling?" asked Sarah.

"I had a question about money," answered Elizabeth. "Mom always knows what I should do. I asked her, and she helped me."

"That is our lesson today," said Mrs. Day. "We all need to ask for counsel."

"What is counsel?" asked Juan.

"Counsel is asking other people what they think you should do," answered Mrs. Day. "Does anyone know the name of the wisest king in the Bible?"

"Was it King Solomon?" asked Paul.

"Yes, Paul," said Mrs. Day. "In Proverbs 12:15 King Solomon wrote, *A wise man . . . listens to counsel.*"

"Who should we ask for counsel?" asked Sarah.

"Ask your parents," answered Mrs. Day. "Listen to these verses Solomon wrote in Proverbs 6:20-22, *Obey your father and your mother . . . their counsel will lead you and save you from harm.* Mothers and Fathers love their children. They want to help them with good counsel.

"But someone loves you even more than your parents and wants to give you counsel." said Mrs. Day. "Juan, read Psalm 32:8."

Juan read, *"I (the Lord) will. . . teach you in the way you should go; I will counsel you."*

"God wants to help us," said Sarah smiling.

"Yes," answered Mrs. Day. "God counsels you when you read the Bible. When you have a question about money, you can read the Bible for God's answer. God also counsels you when you pray. Ask the Lord to help you with your problems."

"Well, we have a problem," said Elizabeth. "We do not have enough money to buy the puppy."

Little did the kids know what was about to happen.

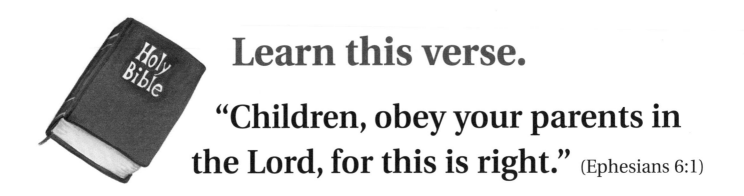

Learn this verse.

"Children, obey your parents in the Lord, for this is right." (Ephesians 6:1)

Answer these Questions.

What does it mean to ask for counsel?

_____

_____

_____

Read Proverbs 6:20-22. What does this verse mean to you?

_____

_____

What have you learned from your parents about money?

_____

_____

_____

Things to do...

Color Jesus with some children.
Remember, Jesus wants
to be your counselor.

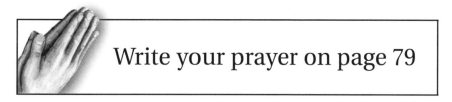 Write your prayer on page 79

Chapter 10

Honesty

"Mom, look what we found!" shouted Elizabeth.

She was holding a dog. "It's not a puppy, but it is cute. And we will not have to pay for it."

"That is true," said Mrs. Day. "But you are forgetting something."

"What?" asked Sarah.

"The people that love the lost dog," answered Juan.

"We would love it, too," said Elizabeth.

"I am sure you would. But it would be dishonest to keep the dog," answered Mrs. Day. "We must try to find the dog's owner. Get your Bibles. We will learn what the Lord says about honesty. Elizabeth, read Leviticus 19:11."

Elizabeth read, "*You shall not steal, nor deal falsely, nor lie to one another.*"

"Hmmm," said Paul. "Keeping the dog would be like stealing."

"Yes," said Juan. "We need to try to find the dog's owner."

"Good, let's pray for the Lord to help us," answered Mrs. Day.

"We can ask the neighbors if anyone knows the owner of the lost dog," suggested Elizabeth.

Later that day, there was a knock at the door. Elizabeth opened the door. A woman with a kind face was standing there. She said, "My name is Mrs. Norton. Did you find my dog? Her name is Frumpy." As soon as the dog heard her voice, she started barking. She ran to Mrs. Norton and jumped into her arms.

"Oh, Frumpy!" said Mrs. Norton happily. "I am so glad to find you."

"How can I thank you?" she said to Mrs. Day and the kids. "You have made me so happy."

"Please stay for lunch with us," said Mrs. Day.

The kids liked Mrs. Norton very much. They found out she had a new baby girl. But she was sad because her husband had lost his job. The Norton family did not have much money to buy things for the baby.

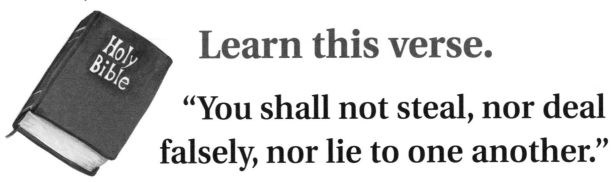

Learn this verse.

"You shall not steal, nor deal falsely, nor lie to one another."

(Leviticus 19:11)

Answer these Questions.

Read Leviticus 19:11-13. What does this teach us about honesty?

_____

_____

Read Ephesians 4:25. What does this verse tell us about lying?

_____

_____

Exodus 20:15-16. These are two of the Ten Commandments. What do they say?

_____

_____

Things to do...

These kids are being honest. Tell your
teacher what you think these
children are doing.
Now color them.

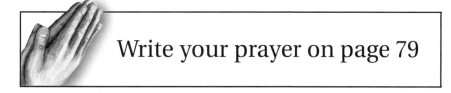

Write your prayer on page 79

Chapter 11

Meet Your Best Friend

When the kids arrived for their lesson they started whispering.

"Why is everyone whispering?" asked Mrs. Day as she walked into the room.

Paul said, "We are sad that Mrs. Norton does not have enough money for her baby. We want to give her some of the money we were saving to buy the puppy."

Mrs. Day's face beamed. "I am so proud of you for wanting to give some of your money.

"The lesson today is about someone else who gave. God loves you so much that He gave His only Son, Jesus, to die for you. John 3:16 says, *For God so loved the world that he gave his one and only Son, that whoever believes in him shall not perish but have eternal life* (NIV).

"God wants to become our best friend. But, each of us is separated from God because of sin. Sin means we have done wrong things like lying or disobeying our parents. Romans 3:23 says, *All have sinned.* But God is holy. He has never done anything wrong.

"Jesus came to take away our sins. He did this because He loves us so much. He wants us to become members of

God's family. In John 14:6 Jesus said, *"I am the way, and the truth, and the life; no one can come to the Father; but through the Me."* Jesus is the only way to heaven.

"We all need to ask Jesus to come into our lives. When we do, God forgives our sins. And He promises that we will live with Him in heaven forever."

"Mrs. Day," said Juan, "I've never asked Jesus to come into my life. What do I need to do?"

"Juan, all you need to do is to pray," said Mrs. Day kindly. "Let's pray right now."

The children closed their eyes as Juan prayed with Mrs. Day. "Dear Father God, thank You for sending Your Son, Jesus Christ, to die on the cross for me. Thank You for loving me so much. Please forgive me of my sins. Come into my life and become my Savior. Thank You, Lord. Amen."

Juan said, "Mrs. Day, thank you so much for telling me about Jesus."

"You are welcome, Juan," said Mrs. Day smiling.

Learn this verse.

"For God so loved the world that he gave his one and only Son, that whoever believes in him shall not perish but have eternal life." (John 3:16, NIV)

Answer these Questions.

Read John 3:16.   What does this verse say?

_____

_____

Who is Jesus Christ?

_____

_____

How can you have eternal life?

_____

_____

Have you asked Jesus Christ to become your Savior and Lord?

_____

Things to do...

If you have not asked Jesus Christ to be your Savior and Lord, pray this prayer:

"Dear God. Thank You that You love me so much. Thank You that Jesus died on a cross so I could know You. I ask Jesus to come into my life. Make me the person You want me to be. Thank You for forgiving me of my sins. In Jesus' name. Amen."

Please talk to your teacher if you have prayed this prayer for the first time.

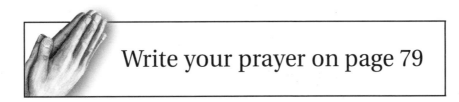

Write your prayer on page 79

Chapter 12

Friends

"In Matthew 22:39 the Bible tells us to *love your neighbor as yourself*," said Mrs. Day.

"You did this when you helped Mrs. Norton buy food for her baby. You were good friends to her."

"And it is important to have good friends," said Juan.

"That is right," said Mrs. Day. "Good friends will help you handle money God's way. And they will help you get to know Jesus better.

"The Bible also says that *bad company corrupts good morals* (1 Corinthians 15:33). This means some people will not help you. Some good kids choose the wrong friends. These friends do not follow the Lord. Always choose good friends."

Just then Mrs. Norton knocked on the door. She was holding something in a blanket. The kids thought it was her baby.

But it was a surprise.

"Frumpy had puppies. This one looks like her," Mrs. Norton said. She took the blanket off the little puppy. "You were so kind to give some of your money to help my baby. I want you kids to have this puppy."

The kids could hardly believe what was happening. The little puppy was the cutest they had ever seen. They crowded around, each one taking a turn holding it.

"God has taught you a great lesson," Mrs. Day said. "You worked hard. You gave to someone who was poor. You saved some of your money. And you were honest. The Lord blessed you because you were faithful stewards."

"Let's name the puppy Steward!" Elizabeth shouted. "His name will help us remember to be faithful stewards with our money. Now let's play with Steward!"

From now on rainy days would be fun!

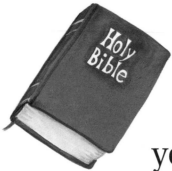

Learn this verse.

"You shall love your neighbor as yourself." (Matthew 22:39)

Answer these Questions.

Read 1 Corinthians 15:33. What do you think this verse means?

_____

_____

Tell your teacher what you liked the most about this book?

_____

_____

_____

_____

_____

Things to do...

Pretend you earn ten dimes.

How many will you put in the **Giving** jar? _____

How many will you put in the **Savings** jar? _____

How many will you put in the **Spending** jar? _____

Write your prayer on page 79

God Hears Me When I Pray

 Chapter 1
Dear God _____

_____

_____

 Chapter 2
Dear God _____

_____

_____

 Chapter 3
Dear God _____

_____

_____

 Chapter 4
Dear God _____

_____

_____

 Chapter 5
Dear God _____

_____

_____

 Chapter 6
Dear God _____

_____

_____

 Chapter 7
Dear God _____

_____

_____

 Chapter 8
Dear God _____

_____

_____

Chapter 9
Dear God _____

_____

_____

 Chapter 10
Dear God _____

_____

_____

 Chapter 11
Dear God _____

_____

_____

 Chapter 12
Dear God _____

_____

_____

SINCE 1894, Moody Publishers has been dedicated to equip and motivate people to advance the cause of Christ by publishing evangelical Christian literature and other media for all ages, around the world. Because we are a ministry of the Moody Bible Institute of Chicago, a portion of the proceeds from the sale of this book go to train the next generation of Christian leaders.

If we may serve you in any way in your spiritual journey toward understanding Christ and the Christian life, please contact us at www.moodypublishers.com.

"All Scripture is God-breathed and is useful for teaching, rebuking, correcting and training in righteousness, so that the man of God may be thoroughly equipped for every good work."
—2 TIMOTHY 3:16, 17

CROWN FINANCIAL MINISTRIES
Teaching People God's Financial Principles

In September 2000, Christian Financial Concepts and Crown Minstries of Orlando, Florida were brought together in the ministry marriage now known as Crown Financial Ministries.

The union of these two ministries created an alliance that is having far-reaching impact on the church in America and around the world. The purpose of the ministry is to teach people God's financial principles in order to know Christ more intimately and to be free to serve Him.